CLARA
BARTON

FOUNDER OF THE AMERICAN RED CROSS

SPECIAL LIVES IN HISTORY THAT BECOME

Signature LIVES

CLARA
BARTON
FOUNDER OF THE AMERICAN RED CROSS

Barbara A. Somervill

Content Adviser: Annie Bartholomew,
Collection Manager, American Red Cross
National Headquarters, Washington, D.C.

Reading Adviser: Rosemary G. Palmer, Ph.D.,
Department of Literacy, College of Education,
Boise State University

Compass Point Books ✛ Minneapolis, Minnesota

Compass Point Books
3109 West 50th Street, #115
Minneapolis, MN 55410

Visit Compass Point Books on the Internet at *www.compasspointbooks.com*
or e-mail your request to *custserv@compasspointbooks.com*

Editor: Anthony Wacholtz
Page Production: Noumenon Creative
Photo Researcher: Lori Bye
Cartographer: XNR Productions, Inc.
Library Consultant: Kathleen Baxter

Art Director: Jaime Martens
Creative Director: Keith Griffin
Editorial Director: Carol Jones
Managing Editor: Catherine Neitge

Library of Congress Cataloging-in-Publication Data
Somervill, Barbara A.
   Clara Barton : Founder of the American Red Cross / by Barbara A.
Somervill.
     p. cm.—(Signature lives)
   Includes bibliographical references and index.
   ISBN-13: 978-0-7565-1888-2 (library binding)
   ISBN-10: 0-7565-1888-1 (library binding)
   ISBN-13: 978-0-7565-2199-8 (paperback)
   ISBN-10: 0-7565-2199-8 (paperback)
   1. Barton, Clara, 1821–1912—Juvenile literature. 2. American Red
Cross—Biography—Juvenile literature. 3. Nurses—United States—
Biography—Juvenile literature. 4. Barton, Clara, 1821-1912. 5. American
Red Cross—Biography. 6. Nurses—United States—Biography. I. Title.
II. Series.
   HV569.B3S64 2007
   361.7'634092—dc22   2006027071

CIVIL WAR ERA

The Civil War (1861–1865) split the United States into two countries and divided the people over the issue of slavery. The opposing sides—the Union in the North and the Confederacy in the South—battled each other for four long years in the deadliest American conflict ever fought. The bloody war sometimes pitted family members and friends against each other over the issues of slavery and states' rights. Some of the people who lived and served their country during the Civil War are among the nation's most beloved heroes.

Table of Contents

1 BLOOD FLOWS AT ANTIETAM

❧❦❧

It was early in the Civil War, and rumors traveled through the hot Washington, D.C., air. Confederate General Robert E. Lee had moved his troops across the Potomac River. After early victories in Virginia, the South was invading Maryland. The Union Army would meet the Confederate soldiers at Antietam.

Clara Barton did not wait for the rumors to become truth. She began packing her wagon with food, lanterns, candles, bandages, medicines, and blankets. This was not a comfortable ladies' carriage with padded seats. This was a mule-drawn wooden cart, but it served Barton's needs. Her drivers hitched up the mules, and they headed off to war.

Barton's wagon joined the long train of Union soldiers and munitions headed for Maryland. The

Clara Barton's caring and nurturing personality was evident in her determination to nurse wounded soldiers on the battlefield.

> Robert E. Lee
> (1807–1870) came from
> a wealthy Virginia
> family and was the
> son of Revolutionary
> War hero Lighthorse
> Henry Lee. Robert
> attended the U.S.
> Military Academy at
> West Point, New York.
> Lee originally worked
> in the Army Corps of
> Engineers and helped
> lay out the state line
> between Ohio and
> Michigan. In 1852, he
> became the superin-
> tendent of West Point.
> When the Yankees
> faced Confederate
> General Lee on the bat-
> tlefield, they faced an
> experienced, gifted
> military leader.

army insisted that guns and ammunition went first in line, followed by food and clothing for the soldiers. Last in line were the medical wagons. Barton was furious. She could not understand why they would send the means of killing and wounding men first and the means of saving the wounded last.

Barton decided to jump ahead in the line. When the wagon train settled down for the night, she and her men rested. At 1 A.M., she was up and moving. They joined the line of cannons headed to the battlefront. "All that weary, dusty day I followed the cannon," she wrote, "and nightfall brought us upon with the great Army of the Potomac, 80,000 men resting up their arms in the face of a foe equal in number, sullen ... and desperate."

It was mid-September 1862. So far, the North was losing the Civil War. Robert E. Lee and the other Confederate generals had repeatedly outsmarted the Union Army. The rebels had moved into Maryland, to an area bounded by the Potomac River and Antietam

Creek. Union General George McClellan positioned his troops across the creek opposite Lee's army. At dawn on September 17, the Battle of Antietam began.

Clara Barton arrived with her supplies and set up behind "Fighting Joe" Hooker, a Union Army commander known for being an aggressive fighter. She knew the heaviest fighting would take place there because Hooker's troops were usually found where the battle was the most intense.

Major General Joseph Hooker (1814–1879)

An old barn had been turned into a makeshift hospital. Three hundred wounded lay on hay bales, tables, or bare ground. Later, Barton's assistant, Cornelius Welles, recalled:

> *We were entirely surrounded ... by those whose wounds were of the most ghastly and dangerous character, legs and arms off, and all manner of gaping wounds from shell and minnie balls.*

Barton immediately saw that there were no doctors around and went to look for them. She found the surgeons operating in a nearby farmhouse. Barton immediately offered her help.

Years later, Army Surgeon James Dunn wrote:

General George McClellan (1826–1885) attended West Point and became an engineer. Although he had a military education, McClellan was not a good army commander. He waited too long to follow battle plans. In 1861, he reacted slowly to the Confederate attacks at Manassas. By the time McClellan arrived, the rebel army had left. Heavy losses for the Union Army caused people to call him "Mac the Unready."

I was in the hospital that afternoon, for it was then only that the wounded began to come in. We had ... torn up every sheet in the house, and everything we could find, when who should drive up but our old friend, with a team loaded down with dressings of every kind, and everything we could ask for. She [Clara Barton] distributed her articles to the different hospitals, worked all night making soup, all the next day and night, and when I left four days after the battle, I left her there ministering to the wounded and dying.

The battle raged around her, but Clara Barton never flinched. She moved from farmhouse to barn and from shed to lean-to, bringing soup to the soldiers and nursing the wounded. The

Clara Barton tended to Union soldiers who were injured in battle.

number of wounded was so great that any shelter available became a sickroom.

In the farmyard, a soldier lay with a bullet in his cheek. He begged Barton to remove it. Although she encouraged him to see the surgeon, he refused. He said that those with more serious injuries needed the doctors more. Gritting her teeth, Barton used her pocketknife to extract the bullet.

Throughout the day, bullets whizzed past and cannon fire echoed across the fields. Barton wrote:

> *A man lying upon the ground asked for a drink; I stopped to give it. ... Just at this moment a bullet sped its free and easy way between us, tearing a hole in my sleeve and found its way into his body. He fell back dead. There was no more to be done for him and I left him to his rest.*

In the Battle of Antietam, Lee's troops had been caught between the Union Army and the Potomac River. Although Union troops eventually forced the Confederate army to retreat back into Virginia, the cost in lives was terrible. The total number of dead and wounded from both sides exceeded 23,000 men. Bodies of dead men and horses covered the battlefield. The stench of rotting corpses filled the air.

Yet Clara Barton ignored it all, helping as many wounded soldiers as she could. Four days after the battle, she continued to work tirelessly. Dunn said of Barton: "In my feeble estimation Gen. McClellan, with all his laurels [achievements], sinks into significance besides the true heroine of the age: the angel of the battlefield."

That was Clara Barton—the angel of the

The battle of Antietam claimed the lives of thousands of soldiers from both armies.

battlefield, the angel of mercy. From the Civil War to the streets of Russia, from the Johnstown, Pennsylvania, floods to the starving Armenians of Turkey, Clara Barton dedicated her life to helping those in need. She founded the American Red Cross, an agency that continues to be the first line of aid during disasters.

Yet this fearless, tireless angel was once a shy, quiet tomboy. No one could have expected that such a hesitant, bashful child would become a heroine of the Civil War. ✑

2 A YOUNG CLARA BARTON

❧⟨✕⟩❧

The Barton family got a special gift on Christmas Day 1821: the birth of Clarissa Harlowe Barton. The family, which had lived in Oxford, Massachusetts, for many years, called the baby Clara.

Clara's father, Captain Stephen Barton, led his household in a military manner. The "Captain" had served as a soldier in the Indian Wars but never held the rank of captain. Still he preferred using the title, and everyone who knew him accepted it. Young Clara often listened to her father's tales of his soldiering days and the signing of a peace treaty.

Captain Barton commanded the Oxford militia. He had a strong sense of community and served on the town council and in the state government. Later in life, Clara recalled her father teaching her that

Massachusetts landscape in the early 1800s

"next to Heaven, our highest duty was to love and serve our country and honor and support its laws."

Clara idolized her father as a strong, brave, and heroic man. She did not view her mother, Sarah Stone Barton, with the same affection. Sarah had married at 17, a normal age for women to marry in the early 1800s. In looks and manner, Sarah was plump, plain, and stern. She wore her dark hair parted down the middle and pulled back from her face. Sarah generally woke before dawn to begin her daily household chores. She ran a tight, efficient home in which her three daughters shared in baking, sewing, cooking, and cleaning. Her two sons, of course, were not expected to do "women's work."

Clarissa Harlowe Barton was named for a character in the novel Clarissa Harlowe; or The History of a Young Woman, *written by Samuel Richardson in 1748. Richardson was considered to be an important novelist of his time, and his books remained popular well into the 1800s.* Clarissa Harlowe; or The History of a Young Woman *brought sighs and tears to female readers for years.*

Compared to mothers today, Sarah Barton was stern and harsh. She did not allow Clara to play with dolls or toys. Quick-tempered and sharp-tongued, Sarah readily scolded her children when they had done wrong. Clara had extremely tender feelings, and being scolded hurt her deeply.

As the youngest, Clara often felt that her siblings

The birthplace of Clara Barton in Oxford, Massachusetts

acted like parents. Her four older siblings taught and disciplined her, but they also entertained her. Dorothea, nicknamed Dolly, was 17 when Clara was born. She served as both a mother and a teacher for her youngest sister, and it was Dolly who taught her to read. Her brother Stephen, who was 15 years older, became Clara's math teacher. As an adult, Clara recalled, "My elder brother, Stephen, was a noted mathematician. He inducted me into the mystery of figures. Multiplication, division, subtraction, halves, quarters and wholes, soon ceased to be a mystery." Her sister Sally, born 10 years before Clara, took on the responsibility of teaching Clara geography.

Clara's favorite lessons, however, came from her brother David. At 5 years old, she trailed after 18-year-old David to the pasture where the family raised thoroughbred horses. In springtime, the mares and colts grazed near the Barton farmhouse. David tossed Clara onto the back of a horse and taught her how to ride bareback.

David decided that Clara needed practical education as much as book learning. He expected skill and daring in everything she tried to do. She later said:

> I must throw a ball or a stone with an
> under swing like a boy and not a girl. ... If
> I would drive a nail, strike it fairly on the
> head every time, and not split the board. ...
> I must tie a square knot that would hold,
> and not tie my horse with a slip noose.

Growing up was not easy for Clara with so many people watching over her. Her siblings called her "Tot" because she was so much younger than they were, and they teased her because she had a lisp and stuttered. Clara grew up shy, hesitant, and withdrawn. Although she was academically ahead

of her peers, she had few friends her own age. Her
parents decided to send Clara to a private boarding
school. There was no question that 8-year-old Clara
could handle the work, but as it turned out, she could
not handle being away from her family. Clara said of
the experience:

*Like many
children in the
early 1800s,
Clara was
taught at home.*

My studies gave me no trouble, but I grew very tired, felt hungry all the time but dared not eat, grew thin and pale. The colonel noticed it, and watching me at table found that I was eating little or nothing, refusing everything that was offered me. ... It was decided to take me home until a little older, and wiser, I could hope.

Clara never returned to boarding school. The bulk of her education was provided at home. Then, when she was 10, David had a serious accident, and all thoughts of sending Clara away ended for good.

It was the summer of 1832, and the Bartons were raising a barn. David was at the top when he fell feet-first to the barn floor. At first, it seemed that he was not hurt. A few days later, he developed a headache and a fever. Doctors declared that he had too much blood. This strange-sounding diagnosis was not unusual in the 1800s. The recommended cure was bleeding by applying leeches to David's body to suck out the "extra" blood.

For the next two years, Clara rarely left David's bedside. She became quite skilled at applying leeches to her brother's skin. David did not get better, despite the constant attentions of his young nurse.

Finally, the Bartons called in Dr. Asa McCullum, a "steam doctor." McCullum believed that hydrotherapy would cure David's problems. After weeks

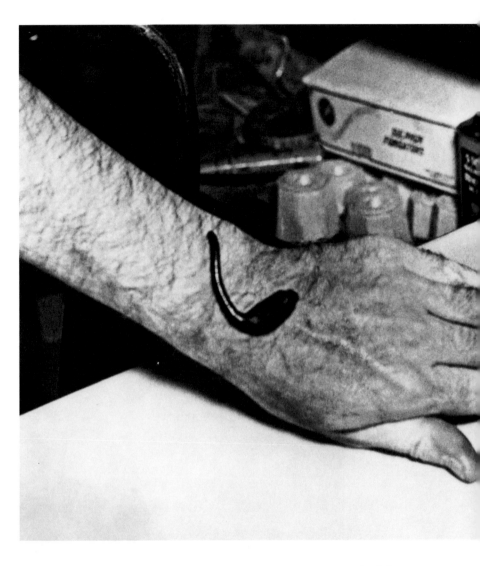

Applying leeches to the skin was a popular medical procedure in the 1800s.

of treatments at the steam clinic, David was completely healed.

Clara's problems, however, were not so easy to heal. Throughout her youth, she remained very quiet and shy around strangers. Her mother hoped to find a cure for what she thought was a personality disorder. She asked L.W. Fowler, a noted phrenologist, to examine Clara. Phrenologists examined a patient's

Phrenologists studied the bumps in a person's skull to determine his or her characteristics. Phrenology, which was popular in the 19th century, has since been discredited.

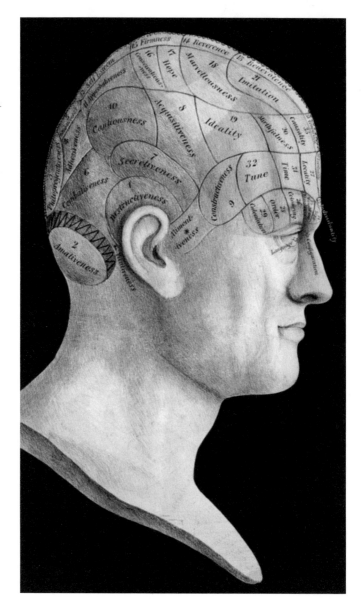

skull to determine character traits and personality problems. Fowler claimed that Clara's skull showed a shy, retiring girl. The solution to her shyness, Fowler suggested, was for her to become a schoolteacher.

Clara came from a family of teachers. Dolly, Sally, and her brother Stephen all taught in Oxford's public school. But in her 20s, Dolly suffered a mental breakdown and quit teaching. She remained secluded in her room most of the time. Sally quit teaching when she got married—in the 1800s, women could not continue to teach once they got married—and Stephen left his teaching job to run the Barton cloth mill.

A teaching position opened up in District 9, close to where Sally lived with her husband. Clara took the examination—a brief oral test of knowledge given by a minister, a lawyer, and a local judge—and passed with honors. She would stay with Sally during the school term.

Barton began teaching the summer session in May 1839. As a short, young-looking 18-year-old, she needed to make herself appear older and "in charge." She wore longer, stiffer-looking dresses, but it did not help. When she opened the door to the schoolhouse, she froze. Forty pairs of eyes turned her way, and she forgot everything she planned to do.

That first day, Miss Barton read Bible verses to the class. After a while, she felt more comfortable and had the children work on spelling lessons and oral reading. She even listened to each student to figure out his or her skill level for the different subjects. She expected to have no problems with most of the students—with the exception of four older boys seated in the back of the room. The boys were set on making trouble for their new teacher.

During lunch and recess, the children started

Schoolhouses in the 1800s usually consisted of a single room.

a ball game. Barton, still a tomboy at heart, joined them. She taught the older boys how to spin a ball to get better speed. She said:

> *My four lads soon perceived that I was no stranger to their sports or their tricks; that my early education had not been neglected, and that they were not the first boys I had seen. When they found that I was as agile and as strong as themselves, that my throw was as sure and as straight as theirs, and that if they won a game it was because I permitted it, their respect knew no bounds.*

Clara Barton's school won an award for discipline. No one was more surprised by this than she was. She rarely disciplined her students. Barton became a sought-after teacher. Schools offered her jobs, some of which she took and some she refused. Unlike most women of her time, Barton expected pay that was equal to her efforts. "I may sometimes be willing to teach for nothing, but if paid at all, I shall never do a man's work for less than a man's pay," she declared. ❧

3 EARLY DAYS IN WASHINGTON

⌘⌘⌘

In 1852, Clara Barton founded and taught in the first public school in Bordentown, New Jersey. Despite her hard work and the school's success, school officials put a man in charge of running it. Barton fell into a deep depression. "I have found it extremely hard to restrain the tears today. ... I have seldom felt more friendless."

Barton found it difficult to think about her teaching, yet she plodded through, forcing herself to work long hours. Although she claimed to feel friendless, three gentlemen were interested in her and proposed marriage, but she turned them all down. She remained single and had no plans to marry. That did not mean she was without love in her life. According to her nephew Stephen:

Barton taught in a tiny schoolhouse in Bordentown, New Jersey.

She had had her romances ... like other girls; but that in her young womanhood, though she thought of different men as possible lovers, no one of them measured up to her ideal of a husband. She said to me that she could think of herself with satisfaction as a wife and mother, but that on the whole she felt that she had been more useful to the world by being free from matrimonial ties.

In 1854, Barton gave up her teaching job and accepted a position in Washington, D.C., as a copyist at the United States Patent Office. In her new position, she made written copies of official documents. The Patent Office was one of the few government departments that hired women. As with her previous jobs, Barton worked extremely hard. Within a year, she received a promotion and began drawing a salary equal to that of men in the department. She was paid $1,400 a year, which angered the men working in her office. Men in the 1850s did not believe women should earn salaries equal to their own.

Her fellow workers began to tell lies about her and call her names. One employee went to his boss, Commissioner Charles Mason, and said that Barton had low morals even though he did not mention any specific events. Mason listened with interest, then assured the employee that he would look into the problem. He added, "Things will not remain just as they are in this office. If you prove this charge, Miss Barton goes; if you fail to prove it, you go." The accusation could not be proved true, and Barton kept her job.

In the 1800s, salaries were very low, and women earned far less than men. A female bookkeeper earned only $500 per year. Dressmakers were lucky to earn $300 yearly, and female teachers earned $250. A female store clerk got paid $156 per year, while men doing the same job got two or three times as much money.

However, Democrats won the election in 1856, and many Republicans who worked in Washington lost their jobs. Barton was one of them. She could not find another job in Washington, so she went home to Oxford. For three years, she lived off the kindness of her family. She did not want to go back to teaching, and every other job she applied for was given to someone else. By 1860, she was on the verge of physical and mental collapse. Yet she was too active and too independent not to have a job. In 1860, some friends in Washington helped Barton get her Patent Office job back, but for less pay.

The United States underwent a period of change between the fall of 1860 and the spring of 1861. Abraham Lincoln of Illinois was elected president, and the South worried that he would free their slaves. The South's economy depended on plantation agriculture and slave labor. Major Southern land-owners owned large numbers of slaves—usually of African descent—to work fields of tobacco, cotton, rice, and indigo. The South did not think its economy could survive without these workers, nor did Southern states want the federal government to have the power to prohibit them from owning slaves. In December 1860, South Carolina seceded from the United States.

By April 1861, the Confederate States of America formed a separate country. The South Carolina militia fired upon Fort Sumter, a Union fortress in Charleston Harbor. Any hope of avoiding war fell apart.

Washington, D.C., sat surrounded by the enemy. President Lincoln sent out a plea for soldiers to help secure the capital city and protect the Union.

Slaves prepared cotton for processing in 1862.

He asked for 75,000 soldiers, and Massachusetts answered the call.

On their way to Washington, troops of the 6th Massachusetts Regiment stopped in Baltimore, Maryland. They swaggered through the city, showing off their new uniforms and shiny rifles. Some of Baltimore's citizens backed the Confederacy and attacked the Union soldiers. Several men died and more than 30 others suffered wounds. The soldiers fought their way back to the train station, boarded the train, and headed for Washington. Once there, the regiment set up camp in the half-built Capitol building.

Barton and her sister Sally Vassall hurried to help the soldiers. This was Barton's call to action. She hoped to nurse wounded soldiers in the same way she had nursed her brother David when he had been sick. She recalled, "We ... came home to tear up old sheets for towels and handkerchiefs, and have filled a large box with all manner of serving utensils, thread, needles, thimbles, scissors, pins, buttons, strings, salves, tallow," and other necessities.

One of the first major engagements, the First Battle of Bull Run, took place in Virginia in July 1861. Back in Washington, Barton read reports that the Confederate Army, was huge, numbering 80,000 men. She wrote, "My blood ran cold as I read it. ... Surely [the Union army] would never have the madness to attack, from open field, an enemy of three times their number."

The Union Army did not have the training needed to face the

The first Battle of Bull Run pitted Union General Irwin McDowell's untrained, untried troops against a large army of Confederate soldiers. Generals Joseph Johnston and P.G.T. Beauregard led the rebel troops, and the South enjoyed a major victory.

The first Battle of Bull Run was fought in northern Virginia near Manassas Creek.

more experienced Southern troops. The battle raged for several days, after which the Union soldiers made a hasty retreat to Washington, D.C. Early reports of a Union victory proved to be false. Soldiers fled in panic. The defeat overwhelmed the Union, and in Washington, Yankee supporters were stunned.

Nearly 3,000 Union soldiers died during the battle. The wounded lay bleeding on the fields, suffering thirst, sunstroke, and hunger. Medical care was not provided on the battlefield but in hospitals several miles from the action. The medical staff could not handle the huge number of wounded soldiers, and there were not enough ambulances to transport them from the fields. There were too few hospital tents and not enough medical supplies.

It was obvious to Clara Barton that the military had not considered medical care as important as weapons, ammunition, and healthy soldiers. She began collecting food, bandages, medicines, and clothing. If the government would not provide care for the wounded, then she would. Although she could do nothing about what happened at First Bull Run,

An army graveyard in Virginia

Barton planned to be ready for future battles.

Toward the end of 1861, Clara's father's health began to fail. Clara received a letter from her nephew telling her of Captain Barton's poor health. She left for Oxford immediately and took over her father's nursing, but there was not much she could do. He ate little and lost weight. It was obvious he would not live much longer.

Clara spent months hand-feeding and bathing her father. They talked about old times and Barton's hope to nurse wounded soldiers. They both knew that few people valued nurses, but her father assured her that wounded soldiers would respect her for her efforts.

Stephen Barton died in March 1862, but Clara never forgot the lessons she learned from him. "He charged me with a dying patriot's love ... to serve and sacrifice for my country in its peril and strengthen and comfort the brave men who stood for its defence." Clara Barton returned to Washington, D.C., more determined than ever to help soldiers. ❧

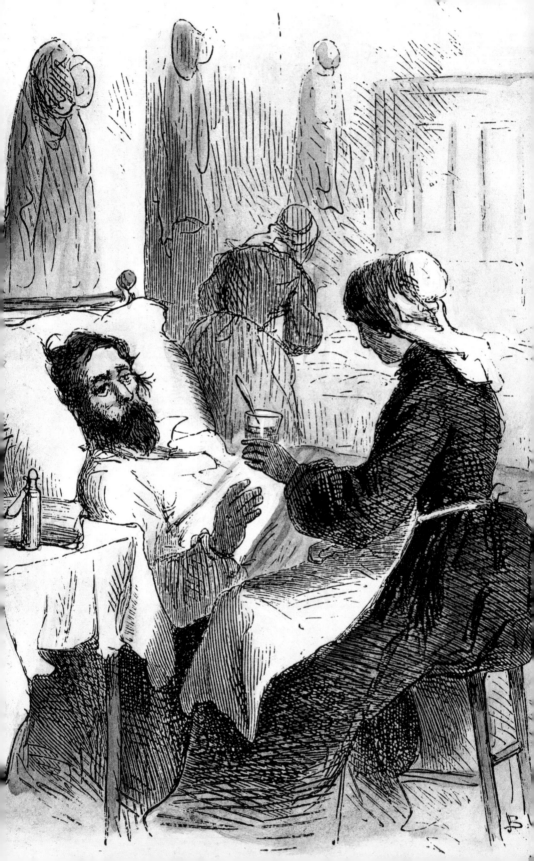

4 THE WOMEN WHO WENT TO THE FIELD

At the beginning of the war, nurses were all men. No one wanted women as nurses—not the military, not the doctors, and certainly not society. Women were considered too weak and too sensitive to nurse injured soldiers. It simply was not proper. Plus, female nurses were not trusted.

Most military men did not realize the importance of proper sanitation and clean water for their troops. They did not think about adding fruits and vegetables to food supplies. As a result, soldiers suffered from diarrhea, malnutrition, and body lice. Few men could survive the conditions they had to live under. So, the thinking was, how could women endure the hardships of the battlefield?

However, an increase in the number of battles

A female nurse attended to a wounded soldier in a Union Army hospital.

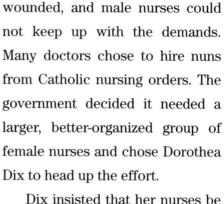

Dorothea Dix was a teacher, author, and social reformer. As a young woman, she taught Sunday school to women in the East Cambridge, Massachusetts, jail. She fought to get the inmates better food and heated rooms. After the Civil War, Dix found that mentally ill patients were treated horribly—chained to beds, beaten, and starved. She worked to get better conditions for the mentally ill. She devoted her life to improving the lives of those less fortunate than she was.

produced an increased number of wounded, and male nurses could not keep up with the demands. Many doctors chose to hire nuns from Catholic nursing orders. The government decided it needed a larger, better-organized group of female nurses and chose Dorothea Dix to head up the effort.

Dix insisted that her nurses be at least 30 years old and plain looking. They had to wear simple clothing, with no lace, bows, or ribbons, and they could not wear jewelry of any kind. Despite her demands, Dix accepted 2,000 women for Civil War nursing. As the number of wounded increased, Dix relaxed her standards, taking any woman willing to perform whatever jobs needed doing.

Clara Barton did not agree with Dix's ideas of nursing and did not sign up with her. She did not want to work in hospitals when so much more could be done on the battlefield. Besides, she did not work well under strict rules and a boss' watchful eye. Barton continued to work independently, following her own ideas of what was needed for the wounded.

News of Barton's work became known throughout Massachusetts, and women from that state began sending supplies, knitted goods, and food. The problem was that Barton was not allowed to go to the field. Instead, she went to visit men in the Armory Hospital on the outskirts of Washington. Although it was a fine hospital by 1860s standards, sanitation and quality health care were still not available. Beds were lined up in large wards where the injured became victims of diseases caught from other patients. There were no bathrooms, the food was horrible, and the opportunities to wash bed linens were limited.

Dorothea Dix (1802–1887)

Barton went to the hospital regularly, bringing treats for the patients. She gave them tobacco, whiskey, pickled vegetables, jams, jellies, and sweets. She read to them, wrote letters for them, and offered them fresh water to drink. But for Barton, it was not enough. She knew that too many soldiers died waiting for help. The best solution was to provide that help at the site where they were wounded.

In August 1862, the battlefield situation was desperate. The Confederates were advancing, pushing the Union troops back. Churches, town halls, and other public buildings were put to use as hospitals. Still, many soldiers lay dying on the field, with no food or water for days. In addition, the military had made a dreadful error by hiring people to take water out to the soldiers on the fields. Each person was to go by wagon with a bucket of water, a dipper, and a pint of brandy. Unfortunately, most of the people drank the brandy themselves, got lost, and never made it to the wounded.

Barton finally got permission from the army to take six wagons with supplies on to Fairfax Station, Virginia. She was eager to help wherever she could. There was an endless line of men waiting for care but nowhere to put them. Many wounded men slept in the open, waiting for medical attention. Others slept on hay that was spread for horses to eat.

More than 3,000 men needed to be evacuated to hospitals for treatment of wounds. Barton was joined in her efforts by women from a volunteer organization called the Christian Commission. Members of the commission brought medical supplies to field hospitals and helped move the wounded onto trains and into ambulances that would take them to hospitals.

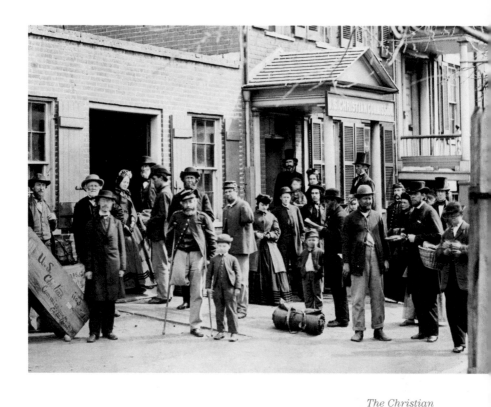

Barton worked for days with very little sleep, staying until the last of the wounded were boarded onto a train. She was determined to be where she could do some good. She said:

The Christian Commission raised more than $3 million and asked for donations of supplies to help wounded Civil War soldiers.

> *I will remain here while anyone remains.*
> *... I may be compelled to face danger, but*
> *never fear it, and while our soldiers can*
> *stand and fight, I can stand and feed and*
> *nurse them.* ✍

5 ONTO THE BATTLEFIELD

಄ೱ಄

It was December 12, 1862. Clara Barton was with the 9th Army Corps camp near Falmouth, Virginia, north of Fredericksburg. She wrote:

> *It is the night before a battle. The enemy, Fredericksburg, and its mighty entrench-ments lie before us, the river between—at tomorrow's dawn our troops will assay [attempt] to cross, and the guns of the enemy will sweep those frail bridges at every breath.*

The day of the battle found Barton at Lacy House, a plantation mansion. Rebel forces had destroyed most of the bridges across the Rappahannock River, but the Yankees tried stretching pontoon bridges over

A U.S. baggage train carrying supplies headed to Falmouth, Virginia, on January 3, 1863.

the river so that the troops could cross. Barton watched as rebel snipers picked off the bridge builders, and she realized she was in danger of being shot. Bullets flew in both directions, woodwork splintered, and glass shards burst from the windows.

The United States Congress formed a Joint Committee on the Conduct of the War to look into many problems connected to the war: illegal trade with Southern states, Union Army hospitals and medical treatment, supply contracts, and reasons for losing battles. This committee was formed just after the Union Army suffered an embarrassing defeat in the Battle of Ball's Bluff.

Her drivers hitched up the mules during a lull in the fighting. As they crossed, the bridge swayed beneath the weight of the wagon. Stray bullets whizzed by Barton and her crew as they headed across the bridge to the battlefield.

Fredericksburg was in chaos as cannon fire and bullets ripped through the town. Roofs caved in and chimneys toppled over. People ran for cover through the streets as bricks flew through the air. Wooden buildings burst into flames. Although Barton knew she faced danger, she was ready to bring nursing help to the wounded on the field.

Barton brought food, medicine, and bandages to the wounded soldiers. She gave water to the thirsty and fed the hungry. Within two days, Lacy House had become a makeshift hospital. Wounded soldiers crowded into the rooms, halls, and stairwells.

Barton nursed the wounded tirelessly for two solid weeks. As she worked, she noted the need for more beds, better shelter, and ambulances. She returned to Washington to beg Congress to improve medical care for the wounded. She wanted better hospitals and ambulances, as well as improved training and supplies for the medical corps. Few politicians could refuse Barton's pleas.

By 1863, the U.S. Sanitary Commission's nursing corps was fully organized and at work. The Sanitary Commission was a privately run agency that provided

Beds were lined up close together to make room for the increasing number of wounded soldiers.

nursing staff for field hospitals, similar to what Barton was doing independently. The commission was dedicated to improving healthful conditions for Union soldiers. Many of the women active in the commission later became activists for women's rights.

The war headed southward, and the Union Army moved into the sweltering, sticky humidity of Carolina's Sea Islands. The war had begun with cannon fire on Fort Sumter in Charleston, South Carolina. The city became a source of irritation to the Yankees, and the Union wanted Fort Sumter back.

In May, Barton joined her brother David, now a captain in the Union Army. He was posted at Hilton Head, South Carolina. Clara wrote:

> *When I left Washington every one said it boded no peace; it was a bad omen for me to start. ... This P.M. we neared the dock at Hilton Head and the boat came alongside and boarded us instantly. The first word was, "The first gun is to be fired upon Charleston this P.M. at three o'clock."*

Troops boarded the ships and headed off toward the city, but the plan to retake Charleston had serious problems. The Union had too few men, too few ships, and too little firepower. According to Barton, the plan was a disaster. The men soon returned, and it was finally decided that Fort Sumter could only be taken by a combined land-sea effort.

A plan arose to take South Carolina's Fort Wagner instead. On July 11, 1863, Union cannons bombarded the fort. The 54th Massachusetts Regiment led the assault after holding the fort under siege for months. Barton set up in the line of fire and treated the wounded.

Union soldiers stormed Fort Wagner under the cover of cannon fire.

The heat and demanding conditions took their toll on Barton's health. She suffered from exhaustion and fever, and she could barely see. For several months, she neither worked nor wrote letters. Some days, she rarely even rose from her bed.

When she was finally better, she returned to nursing. Battles raged all over Virginia. After one battle, 10,000 wounded soldiers arrived in Fredericksburg. Many lay outside with no shelter, while several large Southern homes stood empty and unused. Barton believed that every house should be used as a hospital. She said:

I saw, crowded into one old sunken hotel, lying helpless upon its bare, wet, bloody floors, five hundred fainting men hold up their cold, bloodless, dingy hands as I passed, and beg me in Heaven's name for a cracker to keep them from starving ... or to give them a cup that they might have something to drink water from.

> *The 54th Massachusetts Regiment was one of several African-American units in the Union Army. The soldiers were free blacks from the North and former slaves. Massachusetts Governor John A. Andrew appointed Robert Gould Shaw, a wealthy, white man from the North, to command the unit. Shaw came from a well-known Boston abolitionist family and had prior military experience. The unit formed the front line of the attack on Fort Wagner. Shaw and 250 of his soldiers died in the attack. Their story is retold in the movie Glory.*

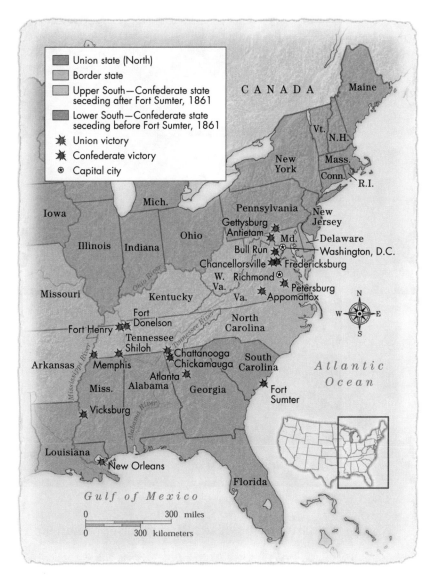

Union state (North)
Border state
Upper South—Confederate state seceding after Fort Sumter, 1861
Lower South—Confederate state seceding before Fort Sumter, 1861
Union victory
Confederate victory
Capital city

CANADA

Maine

Vt.
N.H.

New York
Mass.
Conn.
R.I.

Mich.

Iowa

Pennsylvania
New Jersey

Gettysburg
Antietam
Md.
Delaware
Washington, D.C.

Ohio

Bull Run

Illinois   Indiana

Chancellorsville   Fredericksburg

W. Va.   Richmond
Petersburg
Appomattox

Missouri

Kentucky

Va.

Fort Donelson
Fort Henry

Tennessee
Shiloh

North Carolina

N
W   E
S

Arkansas   Memphis

Chattanooga
Chickamauga
South Carolina

Atlantic Ocean

Miss.   Alabama
Atlanta
Georgia

Fort Sumter

Vicksburg

Louisiana
New Orleans

Florida

Gulf of Mexico

0   300 miles

0   300 kilometers

When Barton heard a Union officer say that Southern ladies' homes should not be dirtied by the filthy, bloodied soldiers, her anger took her straight to Washington.

The Civil War was fought between the northern Union states and the southern Confederate states.

51

*Senator Henry
Wilson sup-
ported Barton's
pleas for better
conditions for
wounded Union
soldiers.*

Barton told Senator Henry Wilson, chairman of
the Senate's Military Committee, about the conditions
that the soldiers endured and the lack of concern of
the officers commanding them. Outraged, Wilson met
with the committee and insisted that conditions in
Fredericksburg be improved immediately. Although
Barton made Wilson aware of the seriousness

of the situation, she gave him full credit for his quick action.

A government investigator rode to Fredericksburg and checked out Barton's story. The story proved to be true, and he ordered the city's food and housing opened to the wounded within two hours.

Throughout the bitter battles, the many wounded owed much to Clara Barton. She tended their wounds and even cooked their meals. Once, when she was camped with the troops, she personally baked dozens of apple pies and watched over the preparation of hundreds of gallons of soup, stew, and coffee. When it came to work, there was no job too small or humble for Barton to take on.

As Union General John J. Elwell recalled after the war ended:

> *I was shot with an Enfield cartridge within one hundred and fifty yards of the fort [Wagner] and so disabled that I could not go forward. ... Two boys of the 62nd Ohio found me and carried me to our first parallel, where had been arranged a [temporary] hospital. ... Clara Barton was there, an angel of mercy doing all in mortal power to assuage [ease] the miseries of the unfortunate soldiers.*

6 A REQUIEM FROM ANDERSONVILLE

Chapter

❧❧❧

By September 1864, it was obvious to most people that the Civil War was coming to an end. The South was running out of money and supplies, and the Union was winning more and more battles. That month, Clara Barton's brother Stephen became one of the many refugees fleeing the South. He had moved to North Carolina before the war and got stuck behind Confederate lines once the war began.

Union soldiers could not decide if Stephen was a rebel or a Yankee traitor. He was accused of selling cotton to buy medicine, and then selling the medicine for a profit. To the Yankees, this activity defied their blockade and broke the law. They took Stephen's money and property and put him in a jail in Norfolk, Virginia. However, he managed to get a letter out of the jail to Clara.

When she found out that Stephen was in jail, she arranged his release. Like many prisoners, he was starved, weak, and in need of full-time medical care. Since the Union had taken over most of eastern Virginia and the Carolinas, Barton no longer felt she was needed at the battlefront. She decided to give up her war duties to tend to her brother. The two of them headed for Washington, where Stephen took to his sickbed.

After a few months, Barton received some bad news. She had remained "officially" working for the Patent Office while she was nursing wounded soldiers. A fellow employee had agreed to take on

The Patent Office in the 1860s

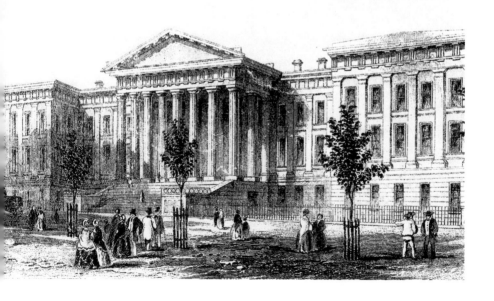

her work for half her pay. Barton received the other half, which she used to buy supplies and medicines. The Patent Office, however, had decided to fire her, and now she no longer had any income.

While Barton was nursing her sick brother, she felt that there was more work to be done on behalf of the soldiers. She wrote to President Abraham Lincoln and asked him for permission to locate missing soldiers. He responded with a letter that would support her in her efforts:

> *Miss Clara Barton has kindly offered to search for missing prisoners of war. Please address her at Annapolis, giving her name, regiment, and company of any missing prisoners.*

In March 1865, Stephen died, and Barton accompanied his body back to Massachusetts for burial. Despite her grief, she could now begin searching for missing soldiers.

April brought major changes in the Civil War. On April 9, 1865, Confederate General Robert E. Lee surrendered to the Union's Ulysses Grant at Appomattox Courthouse,

So many soldiers died so quickly during the war that many bodies were placed in unmarked graves. There were 315,555 known Yankee graves, but 143,155 of them were unmarked. Plus another 44,000 deaths were recorded with no burial listed. In addition, thousands of soldiers on both sides of the war remained "missing." Some had deserted their posts, but others had died without anyone knowing it.

Abraham Lincoln was assassinated while watching a play on April 14, 1865.

Virginia. Within a week, John Wilkes Booth assassinated President Lincoln at Ford's Theater in Washington. The war was nearly over, but the North reeled with the shocking loss of the president.

After the war ended, Barton set up an office in Annapolis, Maryland, and advertised her "missing soldier" services in major Northern newspapers. Within a few days, she received more than 300 letters. After that, roughly 100 letters came each day.

She began compiling lists with the names of the missing men. She put together several lists with 1,500 names per list in alphabetical order. Printing the lists seemed nearly impossible. Printing cost money, and Barton had none. She asked President Andrew Johnson to have the government printing office print the lists. Johnson approved her request, and the first 7,500 names ran off the presses. The lists were distributed to newspapers and post offices, and people sent Barton any knowledge they had about the men.

Barton responded to thousands of letters, and since there were no computers or practical typewriters at this time, she did all the work by hand. Between 1865 and 1869, she answered more than 63,000 letters and identified more than 22,000 missing soldiers.

One of Barton's bleakest tasks took place at the worst Confederate military prison: Andersonville. Dorence Atwater, a Union soldier and former inmate at Andersonville, contacted Barton about the infamous Georgia prison and its mass graves. Atwater's job while in prison had been to record the deaths of Union prisoners of war. This was no small task since

Dorence Atwater (1845–1910)

deaths often numbered more than 100 per day. Atwater recorded each prisoner's name, regiment, and date. He also made a second, secret copy of the death list. When released, Atwater sneaked the second list out of Andersonville. The War Department did not seem interested in Atwater's list, but Clara Barton was.

Andersonville, Georgia, became the site of Fort Sumter prison camp. The prison had been open ground surrounded by a tall stockade fence. The Confederacy provided a few tents or barracks and very little food for the inmates. Confederate soldiers from the 26th Alabama unit served as guards. During the Civil War, there were no standards for keeping prisoners in decent conditions. Many died from starvation, infection, or disease. By the time the war ended, most of the surviving Union prisoners were walking skeletons.

Barton met with Secretary of War Edwin Stanton, who agreed to have the graves properly marked. Then she took on yet another task: establishing one of the first national cemeteries. Barton, Atwater, and a crew of men headed to Andersonville. They opened mass graves and reburied the bodies in individual graves with name markers. In all, they reburied nearly 13,000 bodies. Barton herself raised the American flag over the site.

After Andersonville, Clara Barton reported her findings to the House of Representatives. On February 21, 1866, she testified about her work at the prison. She described the conditions she believed existed in the prison and how she became involved in the

massive reburial.

Barton stated that Andersonville had housed 30,000 to 34,000 prisoners of war who were crowded into a small stockade with little fresh water or shelter. She said that even though the prison was closed, it had obviously been a place of inhumane conditions. She explained:

Clara Barton raised the U.S. flag at Andersonville prison.

> *A slow, small, sluggish stream runs through nearly the centre of it. ... They placed the cook-house and bake-house [at the stream's head]. ... Every impurity from both these houses that was thrown*

*out washed directly into the stream. ... I
saw grease and refuse matter still adher-
ing to the roots of the coarse grass.*

The work of locating missing soldiers had proven
to be expensive. Barton earned no money from the
search and spent her own savings most of the time.
Finally, Congress approved $15,000 to repay her
expenses. She paid off a number of debts with the
money, but she was still just about broke.

Barton thought about writing a book to earn
money, but she quickly gave up the idea when she
realized she might have to pay for the printing out
of her own pocket. Instead, she decided to go on a
lecture circuit. Lectures were popular entertainment
in the late 1800s. Speakers traveled from town to
town, spoke for an hour or two, and got paid for
their efforts. Barton usually charged $75 to $100 per
lecture and gave a discount for lectures arranged
through veterans or military posts. She paid her own
travel—usually by train—as well as hotel and food
bills. Barton's lectures proved extremely popular.
She earned more than $12,000 after expenses, but the
stress of months on the road wore her out.

Barton did not enjoy the endless train trips,
meals in hotels, or sleeping in a different place every
night. One night in 1869, she was about to give a
lecture when she realized she could barely talk. By
the end of the evening, she had no voice at all. Her

doctor recommended that she take a trip to Europe for several months to rest and regain her health. Within weeks, Barton, at the age of 47, was packed and on her way. ✎

7 BARTON IN EUROPE

ംഗ‍ൟ‍ൟ

Clara Barton traveled to Switzerland for a lengthy rest. While she was in Bern, several members of the International Red Cross called on her. They told her about the Geneva Convention and its plans to help the wounded during times of war. One of the founders of the International Red Cross, Dr. Louis Appia, had seen firsthand the horrors of war and decided to do something to help injured soldiers, as well as the doctors and nurses who cared for them. Under the agreement of the Geneva Convention, signed in 1864, armies at war would not attack ambulances, surgeons, nurses, or hospitals. Anything bearing a red cross was not to be harmed.

Barton had no plans to be involved in another war. However, world events changed her mind. In

The symbol of the International Red Cross protected nurses from enemy attacks during times of war in Europe.

J. Henri Dunant
(1828–1910) was
credited as the founder
of the Red Cross move-
ment. In 1862, he wrote
a book promoting his
idea that nations should
create relief organiza-
tions to provide care for
wounded soldiers dur-
ing wartime. Dunant
was appointed to a
committee that looked
into the possibility of
such an organization.
He traveled to coun-
tries throughout
Europe, persuading
governments to send
representatives to the
Geneva Convention.
He later expanded his
idea to include relief
during natural catastro-
phes as well. He was
awarded the Nobel
Peace Prize in 1901
for his efforts.

July 1870, France declared war on Prussia, which is part of present-day Germany. The war began when a member of the Prussian royal family was offered the Spanish throne. If that happened, France worried that it would be caught between two major Prussian powers. French Emperor Napoleon III insisted that Prussia's king, Wilhelm I, refuse. France hoped to keep the agreement with Prussia quiet, but the news was published. Angry and embarrassed, the French declared war in July 1870.

The International Red Cross committee invited Barton to join them and observe their activities during the Franco-Prussian War. Barton was excited by the idea of a protected humanitarian service. She wrote:

*These men had treaty power to
go directly on to any field, and
work unmolested in full coop-
eration with the military and command-
ers-in-chief; their supplies held sacred
and their efforts recognized and seconded*

in every direction by either belligerent [warring] army. Not a man could lie uncared for nor unfed.

Unfortunately, Barton had not fully recovered her health and had to turn down their invitation. Within weeks, she received a visit from Grand Duchess Louise of Baden. The Grand Duchess asked Barton to go to Strasbourg, which was under siege. The Grand Duchess begged Barton to help her arrange aid for the citizens. Once again, Barton had to refuse.

Shortly after that, Barton received an appeal from Germans in Mulhausen, begging for her help. Feeling

The Rhone and Rhine Canal served as a military post in Mulhausen, Germany.

better, she decided to go with a young companion and translator, Antoinette Margot, who Barton met through mutual friends. As the women traveled toward Mulhausen, they passed many people on the road headed away from the battlefront. The wealthy traveled in fancy carriages, while farming families

Antoinette Margot accompanied Barton to Mulhausen, Germany.

carted their goods in rough wagons.

A great battle was being waged near Mulhausen. Nearby, Barton and Margot joined August Dolfus, the president of the International Red Cross committee. Barton helped provide aid to the refugees and suffering citizens of the area.

Travel was not always easy, nor was it easy to get men to listen to her pleas. At times, Barton and Margot went by train, but that was not always possible. Barton became discouraged by the conditions under which she and Antoinette worked. She wrote:

> *Still in the storm and mud, defeated and discouraged, sore and weak, I left Brussels and made [for] Metz, which had that day opened its hungry gates. After a few hard days' work among its famishing, fevered population I came once more to my work in Strassburg [Strasbourg]. ... But I was only one woman alone, and had no power to move to action full-fed ... and well-placed countrymen in this war-trampled, dead, old land.*

Still, Barton's work became a tour of Europe. She traveled in Germany, Belgium, and France. Everywhere she went, she took charge of relief efforts for the homeless, the injured, and the hungry. Just as she had in the Civil War, she ignored her own needs and health in favor of helping others. She helped feed the unfortunate and collected clothes, blankets, and medicines for the sick. Europe responded by awarding her medals of honor. Queen Natalie of Serbia presented her with a jeweled red cross. The Emperor and Empress of Germany gave her the Iron Cross of Merit. Barton received a Gold Cross of Remembrance from the Grand Duke and Duchess of Baden, as well as a huge amethyst pin.

Barton's trip to Europe, which was supposed to be a rest cure, ended with the need for another rest. She went to London and found English weather cold and dreary. Nineteenth-century London lay under a thick, wet fog, heavily dosed with soot from the many coal-burning fires. Chilly drafts, constant dampness, and polluted air did not agree with Barton's health.

Barton struggled with fevers and colds and suffered through sore throats and bad coughs. Her letters home discouraged her family. She wrote:

> *I am weak, and little things seem such a burden to me that it hinders me from doing many things that would make me more at ease if they could be done.*

In 1873, Barton returned to Washington, D.C., and, at her doctor's recommendation, moved into a quiet home on the corner of 14th Street and F Avenue. She had barely settled in when a letter arrived telling her that her sister Sally was dying.

Barton immediately left for Massachusetts, but she arrived a few hours after her sister had died. In shock, Barton all but collapsed. She took a small home in the Oxford area, and her health deteriorated as it had right after the Civil War. She endured headaches, stomach pains, and chills followed by fever. For weeks, she was too feeble to even get out

London's dense smog was the source of Barton's deteriorating health.

of bed. Doctor after doctor visited Barton, but none could figure out what was wrong. She began writing to famous doctors, listing her ailments. No one could diagnose a cause for her problems. Some felt that her suffering was in her head. They said that since she believed she was sick, her body reacted by showing the symptoms she thought she had.

By 1876, Clara Barton's health had become so bad that she became a semi-invalid, rarely feeling strong enough to leave her bed or her home. To improve her health, she moved to Dansville, New York, to be near a medical center dedicated to improved health. She became a regular patient under the care of Dr. James Jackson.

Barton followed the therapies set up by Jackson. She wrote in a letter:

> *The general means for promoting health [is] through proper food, water, bathing, dress, sunshine, open air and pleasant surroundings. ... Little or no medication are relied upon. ... The tables are excellent and abundantly supplied. Meats plainly but well cooked; the freshest of vegetables from their own gardens and an abundance of fruit.*

By 1877, Clara Barton had finally recovered her health. She was nearly 56 and wanted to bring her European experience to America. She planned to

establish a United States version of the Red Cross. Despite all she had done in the past, her greatest work was yet to come. ✷

Barton worked to create an American Red Cross after she returned to health.

8 THE SCARLET CROSS FLOATS

ᴇᴄᴏᴐᴁᴐᴑᴂ

Clara Barton had seen firsthand the protection the red cross symbol provided, but bringing the idea to the United States was not an easy task. She no longer had friends in government as she did after the Civil War. She said: "[After] travels in strange and foreign lands, other wars, illness and suffering of my own ... I came almost a stranger again to our Government with another work, which I believed for its good and the good of our people."

The government did not agree with Barton. There was simply no interest in an organization built to help during a war. The general feeling was that the United States would never have another war.

Barton approached President Rutherford B. Hayes about signing the International Red Cross treaty. He

The horrific aftermath of the Johnstown, Pennsylvania, flood in 1889 was one of many disasters Clara Barton encountered with the Red Cross.

passed her message on to Secretary of State Frederick Seward, who had no interest in listening to her. He refused her requests, not once, but twice. Barton later wrote: "I saw that it was all made to depend on one man, and that man regarded it as settled. I had nothing to hope for then, but did not press the matter to a third refusal. It waited and so did I."

Barton had to temporarily give up on her plan for an American Red Cross. She would pursue the idea again later. In the meantime, she took several years to educate the American people of the value of having a Red Cross organization.

In 1881, Barton's ideas finally caught the interest of President James A. Garfield. He arranged for her to meet with Secretary of State James Blaine, who knew nothing about the International Red Cross movement. As Barton explained its goals and activities, Blaine saw how such an agency could be of value. Suddenly, Washington buzzed with talk about signing the Red Cross treaty. Blaine provided U.S. senators with copies of

*James Blaine
(1830–1893)*

the Geneva Convention's agreements. The honor of signing the treaty would later go to Chester A. Arthur, who became president after Garfield was assassinated.

The American Association of the Red Cross was formed in Washington, D.C. The first meeting was held on May 21, 1881, before the treaty was signed. Barton had no organization, no money, and no support staff. She held meetings and ran the group from her home in Washington's northwest district.

Filled with hope, Barton also organized the first local branch of the American Red Cross in Dansville,

The first Red Cross chapter in Dansville, New York

New York, where Barton had lived while she was ill. Dansville held its first meeting on August 22, 1881. Other local committees formed in Syracuse and Rochester, New York.

As wildfires swept over parts of Michigan that September, the American Red Cross saw its first opportunity to provide assistance. The organization asked the public to help with food, supplies, and temporary shelter for those in need.

Two years later, the Ohio River flooded its banks. Fields along the river wallowed under inches of water, and homes lay in rubble from Cincinnati, Ohio, to Cairo, Illinois. Barton immediately rented river barges because it was the only way to reach the disaster site. She arranged for $10,000 worth of seeds to replace lost crops. Relief workers helped in dozens of small towns, distributing money and food to the needy.

The Ohio River flood gave Americans a chance to help others. Among the helpers were six children from Waterford, Pennsylvania. "The Little Six" put on a show to collect money for other children affected by the flood. Along the Ohio River, the Red Cross left a signpost marking the "Little Six Red Cross Landing."

Throughout her time heading the Red Cross, Barton did not get paid. Like other people, she needed to eat, sleep, and replace worn-out clothes and shoes. When Massachusetts' governor Benjamin Butler offered Barton the job of superintendent for the women's

prison in Sherborn, she took it. The job paid $1,500 a year—a substantial sum in 1883.

Butler expected great things from Barton. He thought prisons were expensive and wasteful, so

Entire buildings in Toledo, Ohio, were swept away by a devastating flood in 1883.

one of Barton's first duties was to cut spending. She needed to watch expenses while maintaining quality standards at the prison—not an easy task.

Butler was delighted with Barton's efforts. Yet, Barton was not happy with the way women who were not criminals were treated. She said:

> *[Many of the women] are [not] guilty of or convicted of any real crime. ... Yet the poor, helpless, mis-guided, rum-drenched women are sentenced to the same servitude, and are subjected to the same code of discipline and go out with the same brand of shame upon their brow [as the] men of Concord [prison] where every inmate is convicted of a crime.*

Barton gladly returned to working with the Red Cross, a job she considered more worthy of her talents. The Red Cross became the main source of relief in the face of natural disasters. Most notable of the group's early efforts were the Florida yellow fever epidemic, the Johnstown flood of 1889, and the Galveston hurricane of 1900.

In 1888, citizens of Florida called on the Red Cross for help in a dangerous health emergency. Yellow fever had swept through Jacksonville, Florida. The national organization contacted the New Orleans branch and asked for assistance. A group called the Howard Association had women—known as "immune

The Galveston hurricane left much of the town in ruins.

nurses"—who provided valuable care during such epidemics. The national Red Cross paid these nurses to travel to Florida.

The nurses arrived in Jacksonville in spectacular fashion. Since people in nearby towns were panicked by any contact with the disease, the train carrying the nurses would not stop in the infected town. Instead, when the train approached the Jacksonville station, it slowed down, and the nurses jumped out. They would dust themselves off and set to work.

The Johnstown, Pennsylvania, flood came the following year. Clara Barton and 50 volunteers boarded the first train headed into the disaster zone. The damage horrified Barton. She wrote:

> *I shall never lose the memory of my first walk on the first day— the wading in mud, the climbing over broken engines, cars, heaps of iron rollers, broken timbers, wrecks of houses.*

On May 31, 1889, the South Fork Dam in Pennsylvania collapsed and sent 20 million tons of water from its reservoir through the Little Conemaugh River Valley. The flood destroyed entire towns, killing people and livestock. Witnesses stated they saw a wall of water sweep into Johnstown and over the surrounding communities. The death toll reached several thousand, and property losses were enormous. It was one of the deadliest disasters in American history.

Barton set up shop in a tent and used a dry goods crate as a desk. She and the other volunteers lived in Johnstown for five months amid the same horrifying conditions as the citizens they helped. Rain poured down, and mud became Barton's front yard.

The American Red Cross arranged for homes and hotels to be built to house Johnstown's homeless people. American companies donated furniture,

The devastation of the Johnstown flood covered most of the town.

The Spanish-American War (1898) provided Clara Barton and the American Red Cross with their first opportunity to help in a war-related situation. In February 1898, Barton and her associates arrived in Havana, Cuba, to set up soup kitchens, supply hospitals, distribute clothing, and house orphans. Cuba was at war with Spain, its colonial ruler. The United States joined the conflict in April, declaring war on Spain after the sinking of the USS Maine in Havana harbor.

stoves, kitchen utensils, and mattresses, along with other household goods. Large dormitories provided shelter for families, and 3,000 new houses gave families back their lives. Barton oversaw the entire process.

Clara Barton did not limit the national Red Cross' activities to the United States. From 1889 to 1891, Russia suffered a terrible famine. Barton arranged for corn and flour to be shipped to Russia to feed the hungry. After conflicts in Armenia became news in 1896, the American Red Cross stepped in to help the victims' families. Barton aimed to help people in need, regardless of where they lived.

Occasionally, Barton came in contact with people from her past. When South Carolina's Sea Islands suffered a serious hurricane, Barton arrived to help. Four middle-aged African-Americans came to see her. They showed her old scars from wounds she had bandaged during the Union attempt to take Fort Wagner. One Civil War veteran said:

I was with Colonel Shaw, and crawled out of the [fort]. ... We's talked about you a heap o' times. ... We's nevah fo'git it, Miss Clare. ❧

The Armenian massacre of 1895 claimed the lives of more than a million Armenians.

9 FINAL DAYS, FINAL WORDS

❧❧❧

In 1900, the year of the Galveston hurricane, Clara Barton was nearly 80 years old and still running the American Red Cross the way she saw fit. Some people approved of her work, while others thought it was time for a change.

The national Red Cross had grown, and some of its members believed that Clara Barton was far too independent. It was thought that she acted without consulting others and spent agency money without discussing how the money was being used. The American agency decided to set up a board of directors, and Barton was supposed to discuss all matters with them before taking action. It did not always work out that way, though; Barton frequently acted first and discussed later.

After founding the American Red Cross in 1881, Clara Barton continued to manage the organization into the 1900s.

Nonetheless, Clara Barton represented the United States at the International Red Cross conference in St. Petersburg, Russia, in 1902. The host, Dowager Empress Maria Feodorovna, spared no expense to entertain her guests. But while Barton traveled, disaster struck elsewhere, and the American Red Cross failed to help.

Mont Pelée, a volcano on the Caribbean island of Martinique, erupted. Approximately 30,000 people died, and the village of St. Pierre lay in rubble. The survivors needed immediate medical help, food, fresh water, and shelter. The American Red Cross' board of directors decided to offer only minimal assistance.

When Barton returned from Russia and found out what had happened, she was disgusted. She wanted to know why they had not taken the lead in helping Martinique. Barton immediately suggested a change in Red Cross rules. She wanted the president—herself—to have more power, not less. The members voted to make the change, but some resented Barton's actions. They went to the U.S. Congress to complain. Some even accused Barton of stealing, suggesting she had taken or used Red Cross money without permission.

A congressional committee investigated the Red Cross. Barton had always been sensitive to criticism, and now she was in shock. To be investigated for

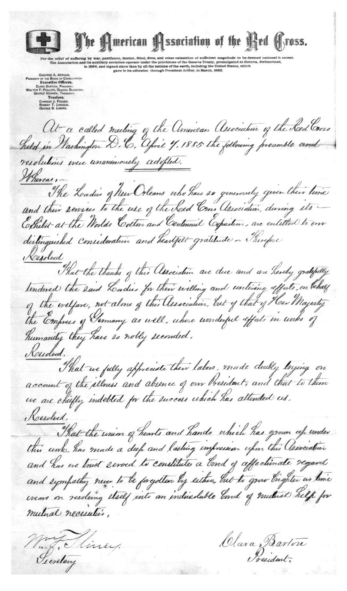

At a called meeting of the American Association of the Red Cross held in Washington D.C. April 7, 1885 the following preamble and resolutions were unanimously adopted.

Whereas,—

The Ladies of New Orleans who have so generously given their time and their services to the use of the Red Cross Association, during its Exhibit at the Worlds Cotton and Centennial Exposition, are entitled to our distinguished consideration and heartfelt gratitude—Therefore

Resolved

That the thanks of this Association are due and are hereby gratefully tendered the said Ladies for their willing and untiring efforts, on behalf of the welfare, not alone of this Association, but of that of Her Majesty the Empress of Germany as well, whose wonderful efforts in works of humanity they have so nobly seconded.

Resolved.

That we fully appreciate their labor, made doubly trying on account of the illness and absence of our President; and that to them we are chiefly indebted for the success which has attended us.

Resolved,

That the union of hearts and hands which has grown up under this work, has made a deep and lasting impression upon this Association and has we trust served to constitute a bond of affectionate regard and sympathy never to be forgotten by either, but to grow brighter as time wears on resolving itself into an indissoluble bond of mutual help for mutual necessities,

Wm. F. Sliney.
Secretary

Clara Barton
President.

Barton was in charge of relief operations as president of the American Red Cross.

wrongdoing, possibly theft, when she had worked so long for others was embarrassing and insulting.

The committee found that Barton had done

nothing wrong, although it did question the Red Cross' record keeping and money spending. The committee did not openly criticize Barton, but she felt thoroughly insulted, and she resigned. The Red Cross offered to make her president for life and pay her a salary, but she refused. After June 16, 1904, Clara Barton never worked with the Red Cross again.

Still, her legacy spread beyond the United States. The American Red Cross is just one branch of an international organization. More than 100 million volunteers support more than 181 national Red Cross and Red Crescent agencies. Red Crescent is the equivalent of the Red Cross, found in Arab or Islamic countries.

After leaving the American Red Cross, Barton contemplated going to Mexico. She thought she could be useful since Mexico did not have a Red Cross organization at that time. Instead, she retired to her home in Glen Echo, Maryland, an enormous place built as a warehouse, the first permanent national Red Cross headquarters, and her home. By

In 1919, after the devastation of World War I, the League of Red Cross Societies was founded to unite the individual chapters. The first five members—Britain, France, Italy, Japan, and the United States—wanted to connect the established Red Cross organizations, as well as help other countries to develop their own. After a series of title changes, the organization is now known as the International Federation of Red Cross and Red Crescent Societies. Each year, the federation organizes more than 80 relief missions around the world.

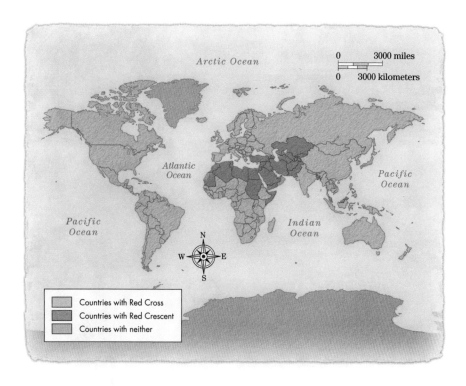

Most countries have either a Red Cross or a Red Crescent organization.

nature, Barton had watched every penny she spent and never wasted money on luxuries. Throughout her life, she rarely spent much money on herself. Her only indulgence was that she loved the color red. Whatever dress she bought was always improved by a red bow or ribbon. In the early 1900s, she had enough money to keep her comfortable for the remainder of her life.

While at Glen Echo, Barton wrote a book about the Red Cross. *A Story of the Red Cross*, published in 1904, presented the organization through her eyes and had a somewhat autobiographical tone.

Clara Barton's diaries, pictures, and other items are displayed in her home, which is now a museum.

In 1907, Barton answered the request of a young girl and wrote a short book about her early life. *The Story of My Childhood* was supposed to be the first of several books that would form a complete autobiography, but this was the only one she wrote.

Clara Barton did leave behind lengthy, detailed diaries. They provide a catalog of her activities, as well as her feelings, hopes, and reactions to events in her life. As a young woman, Barton had often experienced periods of depression. As an older woman, those periods of intense sadness continued. She wrote:

> *I wish I had always remained a little girl. I did not begin like other children; did not learn how to be a child, still less how to be a young girl and woman; and so had no knowledge of the right way to get on in society. ... The longer I live the worse it gets, until now the menacing spirits hover about my poor beset pathway. ... There have been no successes in my life, only attempts at success and no realization.*

For a woman approaching 90 years old, Barton enjoyed remarkably good health. She suffered heavy colds during the winter months, but recovered quickly. In the summer of 1911, she made her last visit to Oxford and her family, but she struggled through a bout of pneumonia.

At Christmas that year, she provided the press with a message for the world:

> *Please deliver for me a message of peace and good-will to all the world for Christmas. I am feeling much better to-day, and have every hope of spending a pleasant and joyful Christmas, my ninetieth birthday.*

Winter wore on, and Barton caught double pneumonia, a disease affecting both lungs. This time, she could not shake off the illness. For months, her health improved slightly, then failed again. On April 12, 1912, Clara Barton died at Glen Echo. Friends and relatives held a memorial service, and the burial was planned in Oxford, Massachusetts, Barton's childhood hometown.

So many people attended the service that it had to be held in Memorial Hall, a larger facility than her local church. Even then, 500 people stood outside the building. Hundreds of floral bouquets surrounded the coffin, and a red cross made from carnations was placed above it. A bouquet of Barton's favorite red roses lay on the coffin as well.

Clara Barton's legacy continues today. When hurricanes strike or forest fires burn out of control, the Red Cross provides relief. The Red Cross stands ready to help with any natural disaster, including floods, earthquakes, and landslides. The agency oversees blood donations across the country. It serves the military, providing a link between overseas troops and their families. It also provides military families with financial help, counseling, and support.

In communities across the United States and its territories, the Red Cross teaches health and safety. It sponsors lessons in first aid, CPR,

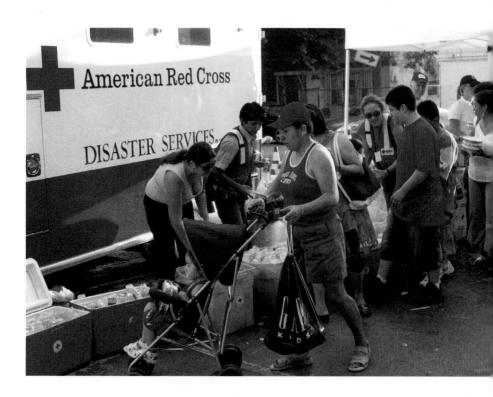

swimming, and becoming a lifeguard. In an average year, more than 10 million people take Red Cross health and safety courses.

This global presence fulfilled Barton's goals. The *New York Globe* offered this praise at her death: "Give the world enough Clara Bartons and the brotherhood of man will be ushered in." ❧

The American Red Cross provided food and water to citizens of Queens, New York, after they went more than a week without electricity in July 2006.

BARTON'S LIFE

1821

Born on Christmas Day in Oxford, Massachusetts

1839

Teaches in schools near Oxford

1852

Establishes a public school in Bordentown, New Jersey

1840

1821

Simon Bolivar frees Venezuela from Spanish rule

1839

Scotsman Kirkpatrick Macmillan completes the first workable bicycle; he calls it the velocipede

1851

Ariel and Umbriel, moons of Uranus, are discovered by William Lassell

WORLD EVENTS

1866

Helps establish the first national cemetery at Andersonville, Georgia

1862

Works tirelessly at the battles of Antietam and Fredericksburg

1861

Helps the wounded of the 6th Massachusetts Regiment after they are attacked in Baltimore

1860

1860

Postage stamps are widely used throughout the world

1862

Victor Hugo publishes *Les Misérables*

1865

Slavery is abolished in the United States

BARTON'S LIFE

1881

Elected president of the American Association of the Red Cross

1871

Participates in relief work in Europe during the Franco-Prussian War

1869

Travels to Europe to regain health; meets Dr. Louis Appia and hears about the International Red Cross

1870

1869

The periodic table of elements is invented by Dimitri Mendeleev

1871

P.T. Barnum opens his traveling circus, "the greatest show on Earth"

1881

Booker T. Washington founds Tuskegee Institute

WORLD EVENTS

1883

Provides relief
to homeless
after the Ohio
River floods

1888

Supports nurses
in Jacksonville,
Florida, during
the yellow
fever epidemic

1889

Arrives in Johnstown,
Pennsylvania, to
direct relief
operations after a
devastating flood

1885

1886

Grover Cleveland
dedicates the Statue
of Liberty in New
York Harbor, a gift
from the people
of France

1889

The Eiffel Tower
opens in Paris,
France

BARTON'S LIFE

1896

Travels to Armenia
to assist starving and
sick citizens

1900

Distributes aid
after Galveston,
Texas, is
destroyed by
a hurricane

1902

Represents
the U.S. at the
International Red
Cross conference
in St. Petersburg,
Russia

1895

1896

The first modern
Olympic Games
are held in
Athens, Greece

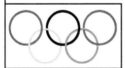

1900

First rigid
dirigible is built
by Ferdinand
von Zeppelin

1903

Brothers Orville
and Wilbur Wright
successfully fly a
powered airplane

WORLD EVENTS

1904

Publishes *A Story of the Red Cross*; resigns as president of the American Red Cross

1907

Publishes *The Story of My Childhood*

1912

Dies April 12 at her home in Glen Echo, Maryland, at the age of 90

1910

1904

Cy Young of the Boston Americans pitches the first perfect game in modern baseball history

1912

The *Titanic* sinks on its maiden voyage; more than 1,500 people die

DATE OF BIRTH: December 25, 1821

BIRTHPLACE: Oxford, Massachusetts

FATHER: Stephen Barton
(1774–1862)

MOTHER: Sarah Stone Barton
(1783–1851)

EDUCATION: Mainly taught at home

SIBLINGS: Dorothea "Dolly"
(1804–1846)
Stephen (1806–1865)
David (1808–1888)
Sally (1811–1874)

DATE OF DEATH: April 12, 1912

PLACE OF BURIAL: Oxford, Massachusetts

FURTHER READING

Collier, James Lincoln. *The Clara Barton You Never Knew*. New York: Children's Press, 2003.

Klingel, Cynthia. *Clara Barton: Founder of the American Red Cross*. Chanhassen, Minn.: The Child's World, 2003.

McPherson, James M. *Fields of Fury: The American Civil War*. New York: Atheneum, 2002.

Raum, Elizabeth. *Clara Barton*. Chicago: Heinemann, 2004.

LOOK FOR MORE SIGNATURE LIVES BOOKS ABOUT THIS ERA:

Jefferson Davis: *President of the Confederate States of America*

Frederick Douglass: *Slave, Writer, Abolitionist*

William Lloyd Garrison: *Abolitionist and Journalist*

Ulysses S. Grant: *Union General and U.S. President*

Thomas "Stonewall" Jackson: *Confederate General*

Robert E. Lee: *Confederate Commander*

Abraham Lincoln: *Great American President*

Harriet Beecher Stowe: *Author and Advocate*

Elizabeth Van Lew: *Civil War Spy*

ON THE WEB

For more information on this topic, use FactHound.

1. Go to *www.facthound.com*

2. Type in this book ID: 0756518881

3. Click on the *Fetch It* button.

FactHound will find the best Web sites for you.

HISTORIC SITES

Clara Barton Birthplace Museum
68 Clara Barton Road
P.O. Box 356
North Oxford, MA
508/987-5375
Honors the timeless lessons of compassion and service of Clara Barton's life story

Clara Barton National Historic Site
5801 Oxford Road
Glen Echo, MD 20812
301/320-1410
Displays information and educational programs about Clara Barton and the Red Cross.

battalion
basic combat unit of the Army consisting of a
headquarters and three units of men

commissioner
an official who heads up the administration of a
government department

humanitarians
people who want to help end the suffering
of others

hydrotherapy
treating a medical condition with hot baths
and/or steam

hypochondriac
someone who believes he or she is sick or who is
unusually preoccupied with personal health

malnutrition
a lack of healthy foods in the diet

militia
citizens who have been organized to fight as a
group but who are not professional soldiers

pontoon
a floating support for a bridge or other structure

regiment
an army unit consisting of two or three battalions

secede
to withdraw from

Source Notes

Chapter 1

Page 10, line 17: William E. Barton. *The Life of Clara Barton, Founder of the American Red Cross*, Vol. I. Boston: Houghton Mifflin Company, 1922, p. 198.

Page 11, line 23: Stephen B. Oates. *A Woman of Valor: Clara Barton and the Civil War*. New York: The Free Press, 1994, p. 84.

Page 12, line 6: Clyde E. Buckingham. *Clara Barton, A Broad Humanity: Philanthropic Efforts on Behalf of the Armed Forces and Disaster Victims, 1860–1900*. Alexandria, Va: Mount Vernon Publishing Company, 1977, p. 31.

Page 14, line 5: *The Life of Clara Barton, Founder of the American Red Cross*, Vol. I, p. 201.

Page 14, line 23: *Clara Barton, A Broad Humanity: Philanthropic Efforts on Behalf of the Armed Forces and Disaster Victims, 1860–1900*, p. 31.

Chapter 2

Page 18, line 1: David Henry Burton. *Clara Barton: In the Service of Humanity*. Westport, Conn.: Greenwood Press, 1995, p. 4.

Page 19, line 8: Clara Harlowe Barton. *The Story of My Childhood*. New York: Baker & Taylor Co., 1907, p. 18

Page 20, line 16: *The Story of My Childhood*, p. 95.

Page 22, line 1: Ibid., pp. 46–47.

Page 27, line 4: *The Life of Clara Barton, Founder of the American Red Cross*, Vol. I, p. 201.

Page 27, line 20: "Clara Barton American Civil War Women." *AmericanCivilWar.com*. 23 Aug. 2006. http://americancivilwar.com/women/cb.html

Chapter 3

Page 29, line 5: *The Life of Clara Barton, Founder of the American Red Cross*, Vol. I, p. 79.

Page 30, line 1: Ibid., p. 77.

Page 31, line 18: *A Woman of Valor: Clara Barton and the Civil War*, p. 12.

Page 34, line 11: *The Life of Clara Barton, Founder of the American Red Cross*, Vol. I, p. 109.

Page 34, line 22: *A Woman of Valor: Clara Barton and the Civil War*, p. 20.

Page 37, line 15: Ibid., p. 41.

Chapter 4

Page 43, line 5: Joan Goodwin. "Clara Barton." *Unitarian Universalist Historical Society*. 23 Aug. 2006. www.uua.org/uuhs/duub/articles/clarabarton.html

Chapter 5

Page 45, line 4: "Clara Barton American Civil War Women."

Page 48, line 16: *The Life of Clara Barton, Founder of the American Red Cross*, Vol. I, p. 238.

Page 50, line 19: "Clara Barton Surmounts the Faithlessness of Union Officers." *Shotgun's Home of the American Civil War*. 15 Aug. 2006. www.civilwarhome.com/cbarton.htm

Page 53, line 17: *The Life of Clara Barton, Founder of the American Red Cross*, Vol. I, p. 252.

Chapter 6

Page 57, line 11: *Clara Barton: In the Service of Humanity*, p. 52.

Page 61, line 8: U.S. House of Representatives. *Clara Barton's Testimony, Feb. 21, 1866*. 17 Nov. 2002. 4 July 2005. www.nps.gov/clba/chron2/cbcongress.htm

Chapter 7

Page 66, line 23: *The Life of Clara Barton, Founder of the American Red Cross*, Vol. II, p. 11.

Page 69, line 12: Ibid., p. 31.

Page 70, line 19: Ibid., p. 77.

Chapter 8

Page 75, line 5: Clara Harlowe Barton. *A Story of the Red Cross*. New York: D. Appleton and Company, 1904, p. 3.

Page 76, line 4: *The Life of Clara Barton, Founder of the American Red Cross*, Vol. II, p. 146.

Page 80, line 7: *Clara Barton: In the Service of Humanity*, p. 103.

Page 82, line 14: *A Story of the Red Cross*, p. 55.

Page 85, line 1: Ibid., p. 80.

Chapter 9

Page 93, line 6: *The Life of Clara Barton, Founder of the American Red Cross*, Vol. II, p. 186.

Page 93, line 24: Ibid., p. 374.

Page 95, line 5: *Clara Barton: In the Service of Humanity*, p. 163.

Barton, Clara Harlowe. *A Story of the Red Cross*. New York: D. Appleton and Company, 1904.

Barton, Clara Harlowe. *The Story of My Childhood*. New York: Baker & Taylor Co., 1907.

Barton, William E. *The Life of Clara Barton: Founder of the American Red Cross*. Vol. I and II. Boston: Houghton Mifflin Company, 1922.

Buckingham, Clyde E. *Clara Barton, A Broad Humanity: Philanthropic Efforts on Behalf of the Armed Forces and Disaster Victims, 1860–1900*. Alexandria, Va.: Mount Vernon Publishing Company, 1977.

Burton, David Henry. *Clara Barton: In the Service of Humanity*. Westport, Conn.: Greenwood Press, 1995.

"Clara Barton American Civil War Women." AmericanCivilWar.com. 23 Aug. 2006. http://americancivilwar.com/women/cb.html

"Clara Barton Surmounts The Faithlessness of Union Officers." Shotgun's Home of the American Civil War. 15 Aug. 2006. www.civilwarhome.com/cbarton.htm

Goodwin, Joan. "Clara Barton." Unitarian Universalist Historical Society. 23 Aug. 2006. www.uua.org/uuhs/duub/articles/clarabarton.html

Oates, Stephen B. *A Woman of Valor: Clara Barton and The Civil War*. New York: The Free Press, 1994.

Pryor, Elizabeth Brown. *Clara Barton: Professional Angel*. Philadelphia: University of Pennsylvania Press, 1987.

U.S. House of Representatives. *Clara Barton's Testimony, Feb. 21, 1866*. 17 Nov. 2002. 4 July 2005. www.nps.gov/clba/chron2/cbcongress.htm

Barbara A. Somervill has been writing for more than 30 years. She has written newspaper and magazine articles, video scripts, and books for children. She enjoys writing about history, science, and investigating people's lives for biographies. Ms. Somervill lives with her husband in South Carolina.

Image Credits